FOREX TRADING STRATEGIES

A beginner's Guide to Navigating the Currency Market

ROBERT T. MAXIM

Copyright©2024 Robert T. Maxim

All Rights Reserved

TABLE OF CONTENTS

INTRODUCTION...7

CHAPTER 1. UNDERSTANDING THE FOREX MARKET.. 11
    What is Forex Trading?........................... 11
    Market Participants and Their Roles...... 14
    Major Currency Pairs and Crosses.......... 19
    Market Hours and Sessions..................... 24

CHAPTER 2. FUNDAMENTAL CONCEPTS OF FOREX TRADING.. 29
    Basics of Currency Exchange Rates........ 29
    Factors Influencing Exchange Rates....... 34
    Economic Indicators and Their Impact... 39

Central Banks and Interest Rates........... 45

CHAPTER 3. FOUNDATION OF FOREX TRADING STRATEGIES............................. 53

CHAPTER 4. TECHNICAL ANALYSIS IN FOREX 59

Principles of Technical Analysis.............. 59
Chart Types and Timeframes.................. 65
Common Technical Indicators................ 72
Chart Patterns and Trends..................... 77

CHAPTER 5. RISK MANAGEMENT IN FOREX. 83

Importance of Risk Management........... 83
Position Sizing and Leverage.................. 86
Stop Loss and Take Profit Strategies....... 90
Managing Emotions and Psychology...... 94

CHAPTER 6. DEVELOPING A TRADING PLAN. 99

Setting Trading Goals............................ 99
Creating a Trading Strategy.................. 103
Backtesting and Optimization.............. 107
Reviewing and Adapting Strategies...... 113

CONCLUSION... 119

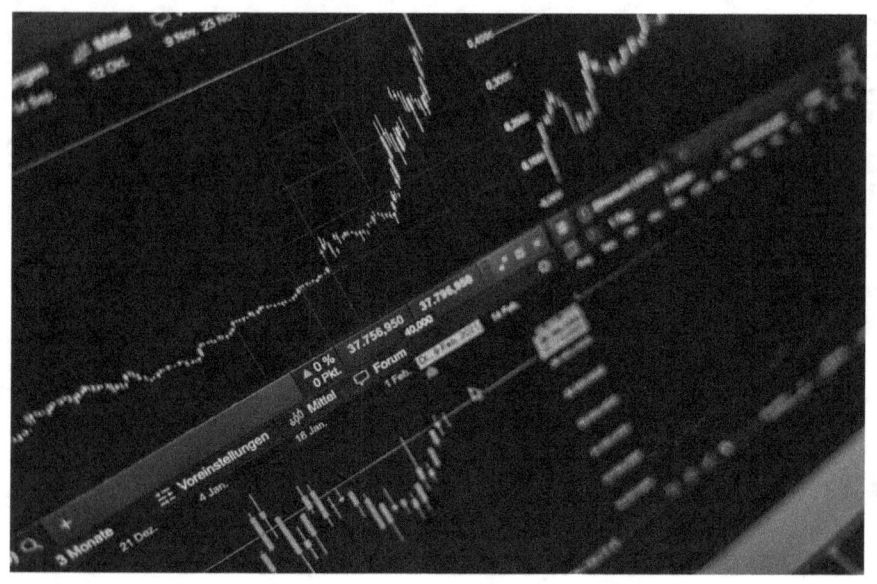

INTRODUCTION

In the bustling metropolis of financial markets, where currencies danced to the rhythm of global events and economic data, a group of aspiring traders sought to navigate the intricate world of Forex trading strategies. The city's skyline was adorned with skyscrapers housing banks, hedge funds, and individual traders, each striving to master the art of trading currencies for profit.

Among these traders was Alex, a young investor with dreams as towering as the buildings that surrounded him. Eager to make his mark in the world of Forex, he embarked on a journey of discovery, seeking out the most effective strategies to tame the wild fluctuations of the currency markets.

As he ventured deeper into the realm of Forex trading, Alex encountered a diverse cast of traders - each with their own unique approach to the markets. Some swore by the simplicity of trend-following strategies, riding the waves of momentum to capture profits. Others delved into the realms of technical analysis, deciphering complex chart patterns and indicators to predict price movements.

In his quest for knowledge, Alex learned about the importance of risk management - a vital lesson echoed by a seasoned trader named Sarah, who shared her wisdom on preserving capital and weathering market storms. Armed with this newfound insight, Alex began to appreciate the delicate balance between risk and reward in the world of currency trading.

Among the shadows of the trading floor, whispers of breakout strategies and range-bound plays floated through the air, tempting Alex with promises of quick profits and hidden opportunities. He immersed himself in the study of price action, decoding the language of candlesticks and patterns that revealed the market's secrets.

As the sun set on the cityscape, casting long shadows over the trading desks, Alex reflected on his journey so far. From the peaks of euphoria to the valleys of despair, he had tasted the bitter and the sweet that trading had to offer. Through perseverance and a thirst for knowledge, he began to carve out his own path in the labyrinthine world of Forex trading strategies.

With each trade executed and each lesson learned, Alex moved closer to mastering the art of trading currencies.

The journey was far from over, filled with twists and turns, triumphs and setbacks. Yet, armed with determination and a growing arsenal of strategies, he stood ready to face the challenges that lay ahead in the ever-evolving landscape of Forex trading.

Thus, in the city where fortunes were won and lost in the blink of an eye, Alex's story was just beginning - a tale of ambition, perseverance, and the unyielding pursuit of success in the world of Forex trading strategies.

CHAPTER 1. UNDERSTANDING THE FOREX MARKET

What is Forex Trading?

The world of Forex trading, also known as foreign exchange or FX trading, is a dynamic and decentralized marketplace where traders exchange one currency for another with the aim of profiting from fluctuations in exchange rates. At its core, Forex trading involves the buying and selling of currency pairs, where one currency is exchanged for another based on their relative values.

Unlike traditional stock markets, the Forex market operates 24 hours a day, five days a week, spanning across different time zones and continents. This continuous nature of trading allows investors to react quickly to global events and news that impact currency values. The Forex market is known for its high liquidity, with trillions of dollars traded every day, making it one of the largest financial markets in the world.

The exchange rate, which shows how much one currency is worth in relation to another, is one of the fundamental ideas in forex trading. Exchange rates are subject to fluctuations due to several factors such as interest rates, market sentiment, geopolitical events, and economic data.

Participants in the Forex market range from individual retail traders to large financial institutions, central banks, and multinational corporations. Retail traders access the market through online brokers who provide a platform for executing trades and access to real-time market data. Traders can choose from a wide range of currency pairs, including major pairs like EUR/USD, GBP/JPY, and USD/JPY, as well as minor and exotic pairs.

Forex trading offers traders the potential for both short-term and long-term profits, depending on their trading style and strategies. Some traders focus on technical analysis, using charts, indicators, and patterns to identify trends and entry/exit points. Others employ fundamental analysis, which involves evaluating economic data, news events, and central bank policies to make trading decisions.

Given how unpredictable and volatile the Forex market can be, risk management is an essential component of trading. Traders often use stop-loss orders to limit potential losses and position sizing techniques to control the amount of capital risked on each trade. Additionally, disciplined trading practices, emotional control, and continuous learning are essential for long-term success in the Forex market.

Forex trading provides a platform for individuals and institutions to participate in the global currency markets, offering opportunities for profit through speculation on currency exchange rate movements. With its high liquidity, accessibility, and potential for diversification, Forex trading remains a popular choice for traders seeking exposure to the ever-changing world of global finance.

Market Participants and Their Roles

In the vast ecosystem of financial markets, various participants play pivotal roles in determining the dynamics of trading activities and influencing price movements. These market participants encompass a diverse range of entities, from individual traders to large financial institutions, each contributing to the overall functioning and liquidity of the market.

At the heart of the market lie individual retail traders, who comprise a significant portion of the trading population. Retail traders typically trade through online platforms provided by brokers, engaging in buying and selling various financial instruments such as currencies, stocks, commodities, and derivatives. They often base their trading decisions on technical and fundamental analysis, seeking to profit from short-term price movements or longer-term trends.

Institutional traders represent another crucial segment of market participants, including commercial banks, investment banks, hedge funds, pension funds, and asset management firms. These institutions trade on behalf of their clients or proprietary funds, often executing large-volume trades that can influence market prices. Institutional traders leverage their expertise, resources, and access to research to make informed investment decisions and manage diverse portfolios.

Central banks play a unique and influential role in financial markets, with responsibilities that extend beyond monetary policy to interventions in currency markets. Central banks regulate money supply, interest rates, and inflation, using tools such as open market operations and reserve requirements to achieve their objectives. Through interventions in the foreign exchange market, central banks can influence currency values and stabilize exchange rates.

Another key group of market participants includes commercial entities engaged in international trade, import-export businesses, and multinational corporations. These entities participate in the foreign exchange market to hedge currency risk, facilitate cross-border transactions, and manage exposure to fluctuations in exchange rates. By engaging in currency conversion and hedging strategies, commercial participants mitigate risks associated with international commerce.

Market makers and liquidity providers play a critical role in ensuring market efficiency and price stability. Market makers quote bid and ask prices for financial instruments, creating a middle ground for buyers and sellers to execute trades. By providing liquidity to the market, market makers facilitate smooth transactions and reduce price volatility, contributing to a fair and orderly trading environment.

Regulators and regulatory bodies also form an integral part of the financial market ecosystem, overseeing compliance with rules and regulations, maintaining market integrity, and safeguarding investor interests. Regulatory authorities enforce transparency, regulate trading activities, and monitor market participants to prevent fraud, manipulation, and misconduct. Their oversight helps maintain confidence in the financial markets and protect the stability of the overall financial system.

Market participants encompass a diverse array of individuals, institutions, and entities that collectively shape the dynamics of financial markets through their trading activities, investments, and regulatory oversight. By interacting with each other in a complex web of transactions, these participants contribute to the liquidity, efficiency, and integrity of the markets, guiding the flow of capital and resources across the global financial landscape.

Major Currency Pairs and Crosses

In the dynamic world of foreign exchange trading, major currency pairs and crosses form the cornerstone of the Forex market, representing the most actively traded currency combinations that drive price movements and trading volume. These currency pairs are instrumental in determining exchange rates and influencing global financial flows, serving as essential instruments for traders and investors seeking exposure to various economies and regions.

Major currency pairs consist of the most widely traded currencies in the world, with the US Dollar (USD) playing a pivotal role as the base or quote currency in these pairs. The major currency pairs include:

EUR/USD (Euro/US Dollar): This pair represents the Eurozone's single currency (Euro) against the US Dollar. It is one of the most liquid and heavily traded currency pairs in the Forex market, reflecting the economic performance and monetary policies of the Eurozone and the United States.

USD/JPY (US Dollar/Japanese Yen): The USD/JPY pair is a popular currency pair that reflects the exchange rate between the US Dollar and the Japanese Yen. It is influenced by factors such as interest rate differentials, economic indicators, and market sentiment.

GBP/USD (British Pound/US Dollar): The GBP/USD pair, also known as Cable, represents the exchange rate between the British Pound Sterling and the US Dollar. Traders closely monitor this pair for insights into the UK economy and global market trends.

USD/CHF (US Dollar/Swiss Franc): The USD/CHF pair showcases the exchange rate between the US Dollar and the Swiss Franc. Known for its safe-haven status, the Swiss Franc often responds to geopolitical events and market uncertainty.

AUD/USD (Australian Dollar/US Dollar): The AUD/USD pair tracks the Australian Dollar against the US Dollar, reflecting trends in the Australian economy, commodity prices, and global trade dynamics.

USD/CAD (US Dollar/Canadian Dollar): The USD/CAD pair measures the exchange rate between the US Dollar and the Canadian Dollar, reflecting developments in the US and Canadian economies, as well as commodity prices such as oil.

Apart from the major currency pairs, traders also engage in trading currency crosses, which involve currencies that do not involve the US Dollar. These crosses offer opportunities for diversification and speculation on currency movements without direct exposure to the USD. Popular currency crosses include:

EUR/JPY (Euro/Japanese Yen): Reflects the exchange rate between the Euro and the Japanese Yen, providing insights into the European and Japanese economies.

GBP/JPY (British Pound/Japanese Yen): Tracks the exchange rate between the British Pound and the Japanese Yen, influenced by UK economic data and developments in Japan.

EUR/GBP (Euro/British Pound): Indicates the exchange rate between the Euro and the British Pound, offering a view of the relationship between the Eurozone and the UK.

Currency crosses are essential for diversification and risk management in Forex trading, allowing traders to capture opportunities arising from currency movements across different regions. By analyzing the interplay between major currency pairs and crosses, traders can gain insights into global economic trends, geopolitical events, and market sentiment, enabling informed trading decisions and strategic positioning in the dynamic world of foreign exchange.

Market Hours and Sessions

The Forex market operates 24 hours a day, five days a week, enabling traders to engage in currency trading activities across different time zones and regions. Understanding the market hours and sessions is crucial for traders to capitalize on trading opportunities, anticipate market volatility, and optimize their trading strategies based on the active trading periods.

The Forex market is divided into four major trading sessions based on the time zones of the financial centers that dominate trading activities. These sessions overlap at certain times, creating peak trading hours with increased liquidity and volatility:

Sydney Session: The Sydney trading session marks the start of the Forex trading week, commencing at 10:00 PM UTC and closing at 7:00 AM UTC. While liquidity may be relatively low during this session, currency pairs with the Australian Dollar (AUD) are typically active due to the presence of the Australian financial markets.

Tokyo Session: Following the Sydney session, the Tokyo trading session begins at 11:00 PM UTC and ends at 8:00 AM UTC. The Japanese Yen (JPY) pairs see heightened activity during this session, with markets reacting to news and economic data releases from Japan and Asia.

London Session: Arguably the most significant trading session, the London session opens at 8:00 AM UTC and closes at 4:00 PM UTC. As the financial capital of

Europe, London drives a substantial portion of Forex trading volume, influencing major currency pairs like EUR/USD and GBP/USD.

New York Session: The New York trading session starts at 1:00 PM UTC and concludes at 9:00 PM UTC, overlapping with the tail end of the London session. With the presence of Wall Street and significant economic data releases, the New York session is characterized by high trading volumes and volatility, particularly in USD pairs.

The overlap between trading sessions is known as the trading session "cross-over," where liquidity peaks due to the simultaneous participation of two major financial centers. This overlapping period occurs during the intersections of the London and New York sessions, as well as the Tokyo and London sessions, creating optimal trading opportunities for traders.

It is essential for traders to align their trading strategies with the active trading sessions to capitalize on market movements and maximize potential profits. During high-activity sessions, market volatility increases, presenting opportunities for swift price swings and quick trading decisions. Traders can adjust their risk management and trading approach based on the characteristics of each trading session, considering factors such as liquidity, market sentiment, and economic events.

By leveraging the insights gained from monitoring market hours and sessions, traders can enhance their trading efficiency, capitalize on peak trading periods, and navigate the global currency markets with a strategic advantage. Adapting to the ebb and flow of trading sessions empowers traders to optimize their performance and make informed decisions in the fast-paced environment of Forex trading.

CHAPTER 2. FUNDAMENTAL CONCEPTS OF FOREX TRADING

Basics of Currency Exchange Rates

Currency exchange rates play a fundamental role in the global economy, facilitating international trade, investment, and financial transactions. Understanding the basics of currency exchange rates is essential for individuals and businesses engaged in foreign exchange activities, as exchange rate movements impact purchasing power, trade competitiveness, and investment returns.

At its core, an exchange rate represents the value of one currency relative to another, determining how much of one currency is needed to purchase a unit of another currency. Exchange rates are quoted in pairs, with the base currency as the numerator and the quote currency as the denominator. For instance, the US Dollar (USD) is the quotation currency and the Euro (EUR) is the base currency in the EUR/USD pair.

Exchange rates are not fixed but fluctuate continuously due to various factors such as supply and demand dynamics, economic indicators, interest rates, geopolitical events, and market sentiment. As market participants buy and sell currencies, exchange rates adjust to reflect changing market conditions and expectations. For instance, if there is high demand for a particular currency, its value appreciates relative to other currencies, leading to a stronger exchange rate.

Exchange rate movements can be categorized as either appreciations or depreciations. An appreciation occurs when a currency strengthens in value relative to another currency, meaning it takes fewer units of the appreciating currency to buy one unit of the other currency. Conversely, a depreciation happens when a currency weakens in value, requiring more units of the depreciating currency to purchase one unit of the other currency.

Exchange rates are influenced by several key factors

1. Economic Indicators: Economic data such as GDP growth, inflation rates, employment figures, and trade balances impact exchange rates by reflecting the health and performance of a country's economy. Strong economic indicators can attract foreign capital inflows, strengthening the domestic currency.

2. Interest Rates: Central banks' monetary policies and interest rate decisions affect exchange rates. Higher interest rates typically attract foreign investment, increasing demand for the domestic currency and leading to an appreciation.

3. Political Stability: Political events, government policies, and geopolitical tensions can influence exchange rates by affecting investor confidence and risk perceptions. Stable political environments usually support a country's currency value.

4. Market Sentiment: Trader sentiment, market expectations, and speculative activities can drive short-term fluctuations in exchange rates. Positive or negative market sentiment can lead to rapid price movements in currency pairs.

Currency exchange rates are quoted in different ways, including direct and indirect quotes. In a direct quote, the domestic currency is the base currency, while the foreign currency is the quote currency (e.g., USD/EUR). In an indirect quote, the domestic currency is the quote currency and the foreign currency is the base currency (e.g., EUR/USD).

Understanding currency exchange rates is crucial for individuals and businesses engaged in international commerce, travel, and investment. By staying informed about exchange rate movements, factors influencing currency values, and risk management strategies, market participants can make informed decisions and navigate the complexities of the foreign exchange market with confidence.

Factors Influencing Exchange Rates

Exchange rates are influenced by a myriad of factors spanning economic, political, and market environments. These factors can be broadly categorized into fundamental, macroeconomic, geopolitical, and market sentiment drivers that collectively shape the valuation of currencies in the foreign exchange market.

Economic Factors

Economic indicators such as GDP growth, inflation rates, employment data, trade balances, and central bank policies are primary drivers of exchange rate movements. Strong economic performance, high interest rates, low inflation, and trade surpluses typically attract foreign investment, driving up demand for a country's currency and leading to an appreciation.

Interest Rates

Central banks' interest rate decisions directly impact exchange rates. Higher interest rates attract foreign capital inflows seeking better returns, increasing demand for the domestic currency and causing it to appreciate. Conversely, lower interest rates can lead to a depreciation of the currency as investors seek higher yields elsewhere.

Political Stability and Economic Performance

Political stability, government policies, and economic performance have significant impacts on exchange rates. Countries with stable governments, sound economic policies, and strong growth prospects tend to attract foreign investment, boosting their currency value. Political uncertainties or economic downturns can lead to currency depreciation as investors seek safer havens.

Market Sentiment and Speculation

Market sentiment and speculative activities can cause short-term fluctuations in exchange rates. Positive or negative sentiment towards a country's economic prospects, political developments, or global events can influence currency values. Speculative trading based on expectations of future exchange rate movements can also impact currency valuations.

Geopolitical Events

Geopolitical events such as wars, conflicts, trade disputes, and political unrest can disrupt currency markets and lead to volatility in exchange rates. Uncertainty or instability in a region can cause investors to move funds to safer assets, impacting currency values.

External Trade and Current Account Balances

A country's trade relationships and current account balances play a role in determining exchange rates. Trade deficits, where a country imports more than it exports, can lead to a depreciation of the currency as it requires more foreign currency to pay for imports. Surplus economies may see their currency appreciate due to strong demand for exports.

Market Supply and Demand

Ultimately, exchange rates are determined by the interplay of supply and demand in the foreign exchange market. If demand for a currency exceeds its supply, its value appreciates. On the other hand, oversupply may cause depreciation.

Technical Analysis and Market Sentiment

Technical factors, such as chart patterns, support and resistance levels, and trading volumes, also influence exchange rates. Traders often use technical analysis to predict future price movements based on historical data and market trends.

Global Economic Trends and Risk Appetite

Global economic trends, such as shifts in growth forecasts, interest rate differentials, and risk appetite, impact exchange rates. Periods of economic growth and optimism can favor riskier assets, while economic downturns or uncertainty may lead to safe-haven flows and currency appreciation.

Exchanges rates are influenced by a complex interplay of economic, political, and market factors that shape the valuation of currencies in the global foreign exchange market. By staying informed about these drivers and understanding their impact on currency movements, market participants can make informed trading decisions and manage risks effectively in the dynamic world of international finance.

Economic Indicators and Their Impact

Economic indicators play a crucial role in shaping market sentiment, influencing investment decisions, and driving currency movements in the foreign exchange market. These indicators provide valuable insights into the health and performance of an economy, helping traders and investors assess economic conditions and make informed decisions based on the data released.

Gross Domestic Product (GDP)

Gross Domestic Product is a key indicator of an economy's overall health and productivity. GDP measures the total value of goods and services produced within a country's borders and is used to gauge economic growth. Strong GDP growth signals a robust economy, attracting foreign investment and leading to currency appreciation.

Inflation Rates

The pace at which products and services cost increases over time is called inflation. Central banks closely monitor inflation data to adjust monetary policy. Depreciation of currency occurs when purchasing power is reduced by high inflation. In general, low and steady rates of inflation are advantageous to the value of a currency.

Employment Information

Employment metrics that shed light on the labor market include the unemployment rate and non-farm payrolls. A robust economy is characterized by low unemployment and robust job creation, which enhance consumer confidence and propel economic expansion. An increase in currency value may result from positive employment data.

Rates of Interest

Interest rates are a tool used by central banks to manage inflation and promote economic expansion. Higher interest rates attract foreign capital inflows seeking better returns, strengthening the domestic currency. Rate cuts may lead to currency depreciation as investors look for higher yields elsewhere.

Trade Balances

Trade balances measure the difference between a country's exports and imports. A trade surplus, where exports exceed imports, can lead to currency appreciation as foreign demand for the country's goods increases. On the other hand, a trade deficit may put downward pressure on the currency.

Consumer Confidence and Retail Sales

Retail sales statistics and surveys of consumer confidence offer insights into the purchasing habits of consumers. High consumer confidence and strong retail sales indicate a healthy economy, driving currency appreciation. Weak consumer sentiment may have a negative impact on economic growth and the currency's value.

Business Confidence and Manufacturing PMI

Business confidence surveys and Purchasing Managers' Index (PMI) measures for the manufacturing sector reflect business sentiment and economic activity. Positive business sentiment and high manufacturing PMI values indicate growth prospects, supporting currency appreciation.

Housing Market Data

Housing market indicators such as home sales, prices, and housing starts offer insights into the housing sector's health. A strong housing market is indicative of economic strength, influencing consumer wealth and spending behavior, which can impact the currency's value.

Government Debt Levels

High government debt levels can raise concerns about a country's fiscal health and sustainability. Countries with high debt levels may face pressure to raise taxes or cut spending, potentially leading to currency depreciation as investors factor in higher risks.

Political Stability and Geopolitical Events

Political stability and geopolitical events can significantly impact currency values. Stability in a country's government and policies is generally positive for the currency, while political turmoil, conflicts, or trade disputes may lead to currency volatility and depreciation.

By monitoring and analyzing these economic indicators, traders and investors can assess the overall economic landscape, anticipate market movements, and make informed decisions in the foreign exchange market. Understanding the impact of economic data releases on currency movements is essential for navigating the dynamic world of Forex trading and identifying trading opportunities based on fundamental analysis.

Central Banks and Interest Rates

Central banks play a pivotal role in influencing economic conditions, maintaining price stability, and regulating financial markets through monetary policy tools, particularly interest rates. Interest rates are one of the most powerful instruments used by central banks to manage inflation, stimulate economic growth, and stabilize exchange rates. Understanding the relationship between central banks and interest rates is essential for investors, businesses, and policymakers to anticipate economic trends and make informed decisions.

Central Bank Functions

Central banks are responsible for conducting monetary policy to achieve macroeconomic objectives such as price stability, full employment, and sustainable economic growth. They have the authority to issue currency, regulate banks, and manage the money supply to influence economic conditions. Through monetary policy decisions, central banks aim to achieve their mandates and maintain a stable financial system.

Monetary Policy Tools

Interest rates are a primary monetary policy tool used by central banks to control the cost of borrowing, influence spending and investment behavior, and manage inflation. Central banks can adjust key interest rates, such as the policy rate or the discount rate, to signal their stance on the economy and influence market interest rates. By raising or lowering interest rates, central banks can stimulate or cool down economic activity.

Interest Rate Decisions

Central banks set interest rates based on economic conditions, inflation targets, and growth objectives. Lowering interest rates encourages borrowing and spending, stimulating economic activity and investment. Conversely, raising interest rates can curb inflation, prevent asset bubbles, and stabilize the economy by reducing excessive borrowing.

Inflation Targeting

Many central banks operate under an inflation targeting framework, aiming to achieve a specific inflation rate over the medium term. By adjusting interest rates in response to inflation deviations from the target, central banks can influence consumer prices, wage growth, and inflation expectations. Controlling inflation is crucial for maintaining price stability and ensuring sustainable economic growth.

Forward Guidance

Central banks use forward guidance to communicate their future policy intentions and guide market expectations. Clear communication about future interest rate decisions helps market participants anticipate central bank actions, reduce uncertainty, and influence longer-term interest rates, exchange rates, and investment decisions.

Impact on Financial Markets

Central bank interest rate decisions have a significant impact on financial markets. Changes in interest rates can affect bond yields, stock prices, exchange rates, and commodity prices. Investors closely monitor central bank statements and economic data releases to anticipate interest rate changes and adjust their investment strategies accordingly.

Exchange Rates

Interest rate differentials between countries influence exchange rates. Higher interest rates in a country relative to its trading partners can attract foreign capital, leading to currency appreciation. Central bank interest rate decisions can impact exchange rate movements and trade competitiveness.

Economic Growth and Employment

Interest rates influence economic growth and employment levels. Lower interest rates can stimulate consumer spending, business investment, and job creation, supporting economic expansion. However, excessively low rates may lead to asset price bubbles or financial imbalances.

Challenges and Constraints

Central banks face challenges in setting interest rates, such as balancing inflation objectives with growth goals, addressing financial stability risks, and navigating external factors like global economic conditions. Political pressure, market reactions, and unconventional policy tools also pose challenges for central bank decision-making.

Central banks play a crucial role in managing interest rates to achieve price stability, support economic growth, and maintain financial stability. By using interest rates as a monetary policy tool, central banks aim to steer the economy towards their policy objectives, influence financial markets, and shape economic outcomes. Understanding the dynamics between central bank decisions, interest rates, and economic indicators is essential for market participants to navigate the complexities of the global economy and make informed investment decisions.

CHAPTER 3. FOUNDATION OF FOREX TRADING STRATEGIES

Forex trading strategies are built on a foundation of fundamental principles, technical analysis, risk management, and psychological factors. Developing a successful forex trading strategy requires a comprehensive understanding of the market dynamics, a disciplined approach to decision-making, and the ability to adapt to changing conditions. Here is an overview of the key components that form the foundation of forex trading strategies:

Fundamental Analysis: Fundamental analysis focuses on economic indicators, central bank policies, geopolitical events, and market sentiment to assess the intrinsic value of currencies. Traders analyze economic data releases, such as GDP growth, inflation rates, employment figures, and interest rate decisions, to gauge the health and prospects of an economy. By studying fundamental factors, traders can anticipate currency movements based on underlying economic conditions.

Technical Analysis: Technical analysis involves studying price charts, patterns, trends, and indicators to identify potential trading opportunities. Traders use technical tools like moving averages, support and resistance levels, trendlines, and oscillators to analyze price action and make trading decisions. Technical analysis helps traders identify entry and exit points, manage risk, and optimize trade timing based on historical price data and market trends.

Risk Management: Risk management is a critical component of successful forex trading strategies. Traders implement risk management techniques, such as setting stop-loss orders, position sizing, and maintaining proper leverage, to protect their capital and minimize losses. Effective risk management ensures that traders can withstand market fluctuations and preserve their trading account over the long term.

Trading Psychology: Trading results are significantly influenced by emotions. Successful traders maintain discipline, patience, and emotional control to make rational decisions based on their trading strategy rather than impulses. Managing psychological biases, avoiding overtrading, and staying focused on long-term goals are essential aspects of trading psychology that contribute to consistent trading performance.

Strategy Development: Traders develop and refine trading strategies based on their analysis of market conditions, risk tolerance, and personal goals. Strategies may focus on specific timeframes, currency pairs, technical patterns, or fundamental factors. By backtesting strategies, conducting thorough research, and continuously learning from experience, traders can refine their approach and adapt to changing market environments.

Adaptability: Flexibility and adaptability are key traits of successful forex traders. The ability to adjust trading strategies in response to changing market conditions, news events, or unexpected developments is crucial for navigating the dynamic forex market. Traders constantly monitor the market, assess their strategies' performance, and make necessary adjustments to stay competitive and profitable.

Constant Learning: The process of learning forex trading never stops. Successful traders stay informed about economic developments, market news, and trading techniques to enhance their skills and stay ahead of the competition. Continuous learning through courses, webinars, books, and networking with other traders is vital for improving trading performance and staying relevant in the evolving forex market.

The foundation of forex trading strategies is built on a combination of fundamental analysis, technical analysis, risk management, trading psychology, strategy development, adaptability, and continuous learning. By integrating these components into a comprehensive trading approach, traders can increase their chances of success, manage risks effectively, and achieve their trading goals in the competitive world of forex trading.

CHAPTER 4. TECHNICAL ANALYSIS IN FOREX

Principles of Technical Analysis

Technical analysis is a foundational approach to analyzing financial markets that relies on historical price data, chart patterns, and technical indicators to forecast future price movements. The principles of technical analysis are based on the following key concepts:

Price Discounts Everything

Technical analysts believe that all relevant information about a financial instrument, including fundamental factors, market sentiment, and external events, is already reflected in its price. By analyzing price patterns, trends, and market behavior, traders can make informed decisions without the need to consider extraneous factors.

Price Moves in Trends

One of the fundamental principles of technical analysis is that prices tend to move in trends. There are three types of trends: sideways (range-bound), downward (bearish), or upward (bullish). By identifying and following trends, traders can capitalize on price momentum and anticipate potential price direction.

History Tends to Repeat Itself

Technical analysis is based on the premise that price movements tend to exhibit recurring patterns and behaviors over time. By studying past price data and market psychology, traders can identify patterns such as support and resistance levels, chart formations, and trend reversals to predict future price movements.

Support and Resistance Levels

Levels of support and resistance are fundamental ideas in technical analysis. Support represents a price level where buying interest is strong enough to prevent further decline, while resistance is a level where selling pressure halts further price appreciation. These levels serve as reference points for traders to make trading decisions.

Chart Patterns

Technical analysts study chart patterns such as head and shoulders, double tops/bottoms, triangles, and flags to identify potential trend reversals or continuations. Chart patterns provide visual representations of market sentiment and help traders anticipate price movements based on historical patterns.

Technical Indicators

Technical indicators, such as moving averages, oscillators, and volume indicators, help traders interpret price data and confirm trading signals. Indicators can provide insights into market trends, momentum, overbought or oversold conditions, and trading opportunities based on mathematical calculations applied to price data.

Trendlines

Trendlines are diagonal lines drawn on price charts to connect higher lows in an uptrend or lower highs in a downtrend. Trendlines help traders visualize trend direction, identify potential entry and exit points, and validate trend strength or weakness.

Volume Analysis

Volume is an essential component of technical analysis that reflects the level of market activity in trading a financial instrument. Changes in volume can confirm price movements, indicate market participation, and signal potential trend reversals or continuations.

Risk Management

Risk management is an integral part of technical analysis. By setting stop-loss orders, defining risk-reward ratios, and managing position sizes, traders can control risk exposure, protect capital, and ensure disciplined trading practices in accordance with their technical analysis-based strategies.

Timeframes and Multiple Indicators

Technical analysis can be applied across various timeframes, from intraday to long-term charts. Traders often use multiple indicators, timeframes, and confirmatory signals to validate their analyses and make well-informed trading decisions based on a holistic view of the market.

The principles of technical analysis emphasize the importance of studying price movements, chart patterns, technical indicators, and market behavior to anticipate future price movements and make trading decisions. By applying these principles, traders can develop a systematic approach to analyzing financial markets, identifying trading opportunities, and managing risk effectively in pursuit of profitable trading outcomes.

Chart Types and Timeframes

Understanding different chart types and timeframes is essential in technical analysis for market analysis, trend identification, and trading decisions. The most common chart types used in trading are line charts, bar charts, and candlestick charts.

Line Charts

Line charts are the simplest form of charting, depicting the closing prices of a financial instrument over a specified period. A line chart connects closing prices with a continuous line, providing a basic overview of price trends. Line charts are useful for identifying long-term price movements and basic trend analysis.

Line Charts

Bar Charts

Bar charts display price information in a more detailed format compared to line charts. Each bar on a bar chart represents the price range (high and low), opening price, and closing price for a specific time period (such as a day, hour, or minute). Bar charts provide visual information about price volatility, price direction, and important price levels.

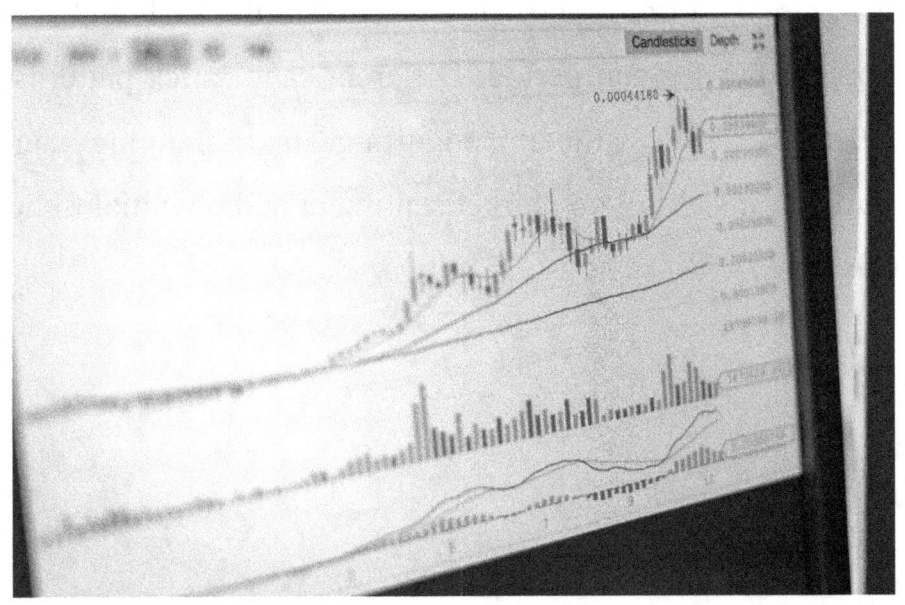

Bar Charts

Candlestick Charts

Candlestick charts offer a comprehensive view of price action, incorporating the same information as bar charts but in a more visually appealing format. Each candlestick consists of a body (the difference between the opening and closing prices) and wicks/shadows (the high and low prices) for a given period. Different candlestick patterns, such as doji, hammer, engulfing, and shooting star, provide insights into market sentiment and potential trend reversals.

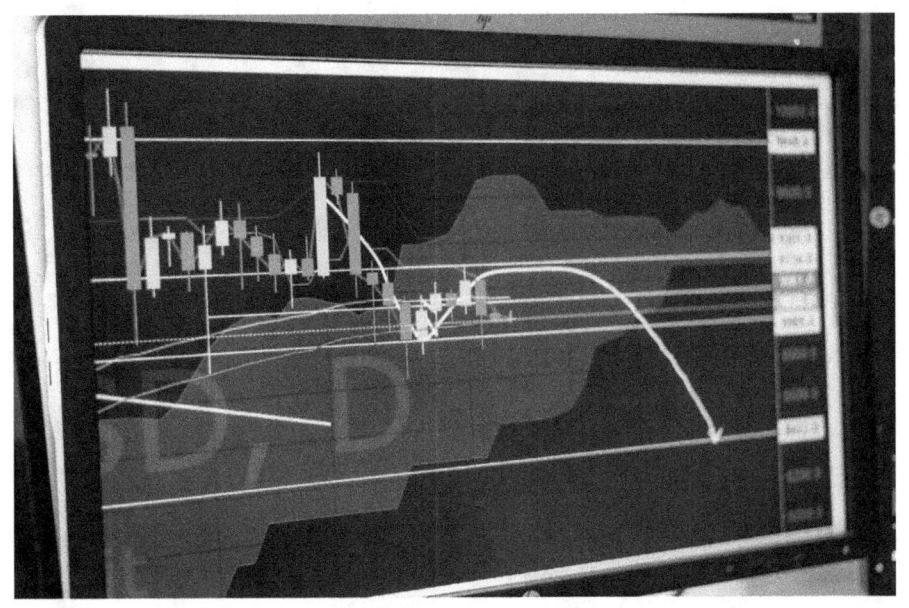

Candlestick charts

In technical analysis, traders use different timeframes to analyze price data and identify trading opportunities. Common time frames include:

Short-Term Timeframes (Intraday)

Short-term timeframes, such as 1-minute, 5-minute, or 15-minute charts, are used for intraday trading to capture short-term price movements. Traders focusing on scalping or day trading often use short-term timeframes to make quick trading decisions based on price fluctuations.

Medium-Term Timeframes (Daily, Weekly)

Medium-term timeframes, such as daily or weekly charts, provide a broader perspective on price trends and market sentiment. Swing traders and position traders use medium-term timeframes to identify longer-term trends, key support and resistance levels, and potential trend reversals.

Long-Term Timeframes (Monthly, Quarterly)

Long-term timeframes, such as monthly or quarterly charts, offer a macroscopic view of price movements and market cycles. Investors and long-term traders use long-term timeframes to analyze significant trends, establish investment positions, and make strategic decisions based on long-term market dynamics.

By utilizing different chart types and timeframes, traders can gain a comprehensive understanding of market trends, price behavior, and trading opportunities. Chart analysis helps traders identify support and resistance levels, trend patterns, price reversals, and potential entry and exit points to make well-informed trading decisions in the financial markets. Combining chart analysis with technical indicators, fundamental analysis, and risk management strategies enhances traders' ability to analyze markets effectively and optimize their trading performance.

Common Technical Indicators

Technical indicators play a crucial role in analyzing financial markets by providing insights into price trends, momentum, volatility, and potential trading opportunities. Traders use a variety of technical indicators to make informed decisions and enhance their trading strategies. Here are some common technical indicators used in technical analysis:

Moving Averages

Indicators that are frequently used to smooth price data and spot trends are moving averages. Exponential moving average (EMA) and simple moving average (SMA) are the two most widely used forms. Moving averages help traders identify trend direction, support and resistance levels, and potential entry or exit points based on crossovers or price interactions with moving average lines.

Relative Strength Index (RSI)

As a momentum oscillator, the Relative Strength Index gauges how quickly and how much prices move. The range of RSI values is 0 to 100; values above 70 denote overbought situations, while values below 30 denote oversold ones. Traders use RSI to identify potential trend reversals or confirm trend strength.

MACD (Moving Average Convergence Divergence)

MACD is a momentum indicator that follows trends and is made up of two lines: a signal line and a MACD line. The MACD line represents the difference between two moving averages, while the signal line is an EMA of the MACD line. Traders use MACD crossovers and divergence patterns to identify trend changes and generate buy or sell signals.

Bollinger Bands

Bollinger Bands consist of a middle band (SMA), an upper band (SMA + 2 standard deviations), and a lower band (SMA - 2 standard deviations). Bollinger Bands give a visual depiction of price volatility and possible reversal points by expanding and contracting in response to volatility. Traders use Bollinger Bands to identify overbought or oversold conditions and anticipate price breakouts.

Stochastic Oscillator

An asset's closing price is compared to its price range over a given period of time using the Stochastic Oscillator, a momentum indicator. The indicator oscillates between 0 and 100, with readings above 80 indicating overbought conditions and readings below 20 signaling oversold conditions. Traders use the Stochastic Oscillator to identify potential trend reversals and divergence patterns.

Ichimoku Cloud

The Ichimoku Cloud is a versatile indicator that provides information about trend direction, support and resistance levels, and potential reversal points. The indicator consists of five components, including the Kumo (cloud), Tenkan-sen, Kijun-sen, Chikou Span, and Senkou Span lines. Traders utilize the Ichimoku Cloud to assess overall market sentiment and make trading decisions.

Fibonacci Retracement

Fibonacci Retracement is a technical tool used to identify potential support and resistance levels based on the Fibonacci sequence. Traders apply Fibonacci levels (such as 23.6%, 38.2%, 50%, and 61.8%) to trace price retracements and extensions within a trend. Fibonacci Retracement helps traders identify key price levels for potential trend continuation or reversal.

Volume Indicators

Volume indicators, such as On-Balance Volume (OBV) and Accumulation/Distribution, measure trading volume to confirm price trends and detect potential trend reversals. Increasing volume during price movements signifies strong market participation, while divergences between price and volume can indicate potential price reversals.

By incorporating these common technical indicators into their analysis, traders can gain valuable insights into market dynamics, trend direction, momentum, volatility, and potential trading opportunities. Understanding how these indicators work and using them in conjunction with other analysis techniques can help traders make informed decisions and improve their trading performance in the financial markets.

Chart Patterns and Trends

In technical analysis, chart patterns and trends are essential components used by traders to analyze price movements, forecast future price directions, and make trading decisions. Chart patterns are visual representations of price movements, while trends reflect the overall direction of price movements over time.

Chart Patterns

Chart patterns are formations that appear on price charts and provide insights into market sentiment and potential future price movements. Traders use chart patterns to identify trend reversals, continuation patterns, and key support and resistance levels. Some common chart patterns include:

Head and Shoulders: A head and shoulders pattern consists of three peaks, with the middle peak (head) higher than the other two (shoulders). It suggests a possible change in trend from bullish to bearish.

Double Tops and Bottoms: Double tops and bottoms are reversal patterns formed when the price reaches a high (double top) or low (double bottom) level twice before reversing its direction.

Triangles: Triangles are consolidation patterns that form when the price creates higher lows and lower highs, leading to a convergence of support and resistance levels. They can be symmetrical, ascending, or descending triangles.

Flags and Pennants: Flags and pennants are continuation patterns that signal a brief consolidation period before the resumption of the existing trend. Flags are rectangular-shaped patterns, while pennants are small symmetrical triangles.

Trends

Trends represent the general direction in which the price of an asset is moving over time. Understanding trends is crucial for traders as it helps them identify profitable trading opportunities. Three primary categories of trends exist:

Uptrend: An upward trend denotes a bullish mood in the market and is defined by higher highs and lower lows.

Traders look to buy or enter long positions in an uptrend to capitalize on rising prices.

Downtrend: A downtrend is defined by lower highs and lower lows, signaling a bearish market sentiment. Traders seek to sell or enter short positions in a downtrend to benefit from falling prices.

Sideways (Range-bound) Trend: In a sideways trend, the price moves within a defined range, forming horizontal support and resistance levels. Traders may employ range-bound trading strategies, buying at support and selling at resistance levels.

By analyzing chart patterns and trends, traders can gain valuable insights into market dynamics, price behavior, and potential trading opportunities. Recognizing and interpreting these patterns allows traders to make informed decisions, set price targets, manage risk effectively, and optimize their trading strategies for success in the financial markets. Additionally, chart patterns and trends serve as valuable tools for technical analysis, helping traders anticipate price movements and adapt to changing market conditions efficiently.

CHAPTER 5. RISK MANAGEMENT IN FOREX

Importance of Risk Management

Risk management is a critical aspect of trading and investing that encompasses a set of practices aimed at minimizing potential losses and preserving capital in financial markets. Effective risk management is essential for traders and investors to safeguard their funds, enhance profitability, and ensure long-term success in trading activities. Here are some key reasons highlighting the importance of risk management:

Proper risk management helps traders and investors control their exposure to potential losses and protect their capital from significant drawdowns. By implementing risk management techniques, traders can limit the impact of adverse market movements on their trading accounts and prevent catastrophic losses that could jeopardize their trading careers.

Risk management allows traders to maintain consistency in their trading performance by regulating the amount of capital risked per trade. By defining risk tolerance levels and setting stop-loss orders, traders can establish clear risk parameters and ensure that each trade aligns with their risk preferences and overall trading strategy.

Effective risk management enables traders to stay disciplined and avoid emotional decision-making during volatile market conditions. By following predefined risk management rules and adhering to prudent risk-reward ratios, traders can reduce the influence of fear and greed on their trading decisions and maintain a rational approach to trading.

Risk management encourages traders to focus on preserving capital and capitalizing on profitable trading opportunities in a systematic manner. By prioritizing capital protection over aggressive trading strategies, traders can build a sustainable trading approach that prioritizes long-term growth and financial stability.

Implementing risk management practices fosters a mindset of responsible trading and accountability among traders. By taking responsibility for managing risk effectively, traders cultivate a sense of professionalism, consistency, and resilience in their trading activities, which is essential for long-term success in the financial markets.

Risk management plays a crucial role in trading and investing by helping market participants protect their capital, minimize losses, maintain discipline, and enhance overall trading performance. By prioritizing risk management practices, traders can navigate the uncertainties of the financial markets with confidence, resilience, and a strategic approach that promotes sustainable growth and success in their trading endeavors.

Position Sizing and Leverage

Position sizing and leverage are two essential concepts in trading and investing that play a significant role in determining the risk exposure and potential profitability of market participants.

Position Sizing

Position sizing refers to the process of determining the appropriate amount of capital to allocate to a specific trade or investment based on risk management principles. Proper position sizing ensures that traders manage risk effectively, protect their capital, and optimize their trading performance.

Traders use various position sizing techniques, such as fixed dollar amount, percentage of account balance, risk-based position sizing, and volatility-based sizing, to determine the optimal position size for each trade. By considering factors such as account size, risk tolerance, stop-loss levels, and potential profit targets, traders can calculate the ideal position size that aligns with their risk management strategy and trading objectives.

Effective position sizing helps traders control risk exposure, diversify their portfolios, and maximize returns while minimizing potential losses. By allocating capital judiciously across different trades and assets, traders can enhance their overall risk-adjusted returns and achieve a balanced approach to portfolio management.

Leverage

Leverage is a tool that allows traders to control a larger position size in the market by using borrowed funds from their broker. While leverage amplifies the potential returns on a trade, it also increases the level of risk and volatility associated with the position. Traders must exercise caution when using leverage to avoid excessive risk-taking and potential margin calls.

Different financial instruments offer varying levels of leverage, with some markets allowing leverage ratios of up to 100:1 or higher. Traders need to understand the implications of leverage on their trading accounts, margin requirements, and overall risk exposure before engaging in leveraged trading activities.

Proper risk management is crucial when utilizing leverage to avoid overleveraging positions and risking significant capital loss. Traders should assess their risk tolerance, trading experience, and financial goals before deciding on an appropriate leverage level for their trades and investments.

Position sizing and leverage are integral components of trading and investing strategies that impact risk management, capital allocation, and trading performance.

By implementing prudent position sizing techniques and exercising caution when using leverage, traders can enhance their risk management practices, protect their capital, and strive for long-term success in the financial markets.

Stop Loss and Take Profit Strategies

Stop loss and take profit strategies are vital components of effective risk management and trading discipline in the financial markets. These strategies help traders protect their capital, minimize losses, secure profits, and maintain consistency in their trading activities.

Stop Loss Strategy

A stop loss order is a risk management tool that allows traders to define a predetermined exit point for a trade to limit potential losses. By setting a stop loss level, traders establish a point at which they are willing to exit the trade if the market moves against their position. Stop loss orders protect traders from significant drawdowns, emotional decision-making, and unexpected market volatility.

Traders can employ various stop loss strategies, such as using percentage-based stop losses, volatility-based stops, technical indicators, support and resistance levels, and trailing stops. Each stop loss strategy aims to mitigate risk and protect capital by ensuring that losses are kept within predefined risk parameters.

Take Profit Strategy

A take profit order is a profit-taking tool that enables traders to set a predetermined price level at which they wish to close a winning trade and secure profits. By setting a take profit target, traders lock in profits at a desired price level before the market potentially reverses direction. Take profit orders allow traders to capitalize on favorable price movements and maximize their returns on winning trades.

Traders can implement various take profit strategies, such as setting fixed profit targets, trailing stops, Fibonacci extensions, and trend-based exit points. These strategies help traders manage their trades effectively, capture profits at strategic levels, and optimize their risk-reward ratios.

By combining stop loss and take profit strategies in their trading approach, traders can establish a structured and disciplined trading plan that prioritizes risk management, capital preservation, and consistent profitability. These strategies provide traders with clear exit points for both loss-limiting and profit-taking purposes, enabling them to make informed decisions, reduce emotional biases, and enhance their overall trading performance.

Stop loss and take profit strategies are essential tools for traders to manage risk, protect capital, secure profits, and maintain discipline in their trading activities. By incorporating these strategies into their trading plans and adhering to predefined risk parameters, traders can navigate the uncertainties of the financial markets with confidence, resilience, and a strategic approach that promotes long-term success and sustainable growth in trading endeavors.

Managing Emotions and Psychology

Managing emotions and psychology is a crucial aspect of trading and investing that significantly influences traders' decision-making processes, performance, and overall success in the financial markets. Emotions can have a profound impact on trading outcomes, leading to impulsive decisions, irrational behavior, and psychological biases that can hinder traders' ability to stay disciplined and focused. Therefore, mastering emotional control and psychological resilience is indispensable for traders to navigate the complexities of trading effectively.

Emotional Challenges in Trading

Traders often face a range of emotional challenges, such as fear, greed, anxiety, overconfidence, and FOMO (fear of missing out), which can cloud judgment, distort perceptions, and lead to suboptimal trading decisions.

Emotional trading can result in impulsive entries and exits, revenge trading after losses, holding onto losing positions too long, or exiting winning trades prematurely.

Strategies for Managing Emotions

1. Develop a Trading Plan: Creating a well-defined trading plan with clear entry and exit rules, risk management strategies, and predefined goals can help traders stay focused, disciplined, and objective in their decision-making process.

2. Practice Risk Management: Implementing proper risk management techniques, such as setting stop loss orders, position sizing, and maintaining a risk-reward ratio, can mitigate emotional reactions to market fluctuations and protect capital from excessive losses.

3. Maintain Emotional Discipline: Recognizing and acknowledging emotions as they arise, practicing mindfulness, and cultivating emotional discipline through self-awareness and self-control can help traders stay calm, rational, and composed during volatile market conditions.

4. Learn from Mistakes: Traders who embrace failure and learn from it are more likely to be resilient, adaptable, and to have a growth mentality, which helps them overcome setbacks, hone their tactics, and eventually increase their trading success.

5. Seek Support: Engaging with a trading mentor, joining trading communities, or seeking professional counseling can provide emotional support, guidance, and perspective

to help traders manage stress, anxiety, and psychological challenges associated with trading.

Psychological Resilience

Psychological resilience is the ability to cope with adversity, bounce back from setbacks, and maintain mental toughness in the face of challenges. Building psychological resilience is essential for traders to withstand the emotional pressures of trading, manage uncertainty, and thrive in dynamic market environments.

By nurturing emotional intelligence, practicing self-regulation, maintaining realistic expectations, and fostering a positive mindset, traders can enhance their psychological resilience, cultivate mental strength, and sustain peak performance in their trading endeavors.

Managing emotions and psychology is a fundamental aspect of successful trading that empowers traders to overcome psychological barriers, make informed decisions, and navigate market volatility with confidence and composure. By mastering emotional control, developing psychological resilience, and integrating sound emotional management practices into their trading routines, traders can optimize their performance, enhance their decision-making skills, and achieve long-term success in the financial markets.

CHAPTER 6. DEVELOPING A TRADING PLAN

Setting Trading Goals

Setting trading goals is a foundational step in developing a structured and effective trading plan that guides traders towards achieving their desired outcomes, enhancing performance, and fostering long-term success in the financial markets. Trading goals serve as a roadmap for traders, providing direction, motivation, and a framework for making informed decisions and pursuing strategic objectives in their trading activities.

Importance of Setting Trading Goals

Establishing clear, specific, and measurable trading goals is essential for traders to clarify their intentions, define success criteria, and track progress towards achieving their desired outcomes. Trading goals help traders focus their efforts, prioritize tasks, and stay disciplined in their trading approach, regardless of market conditions or challenges that may arise.

Types of Trading Goals

1. Profitability Goals: These goals focus on achieving a certain level of profitability, consistent returns, or financial targets within a specified timeframe. Profitability goals help traders gauge their trading performance, measure success, and assess the effectiveness of their trading strategies.

2. Risk Management Goals: Risk management goals involve setting parameters for managing risk exposure, protecting capital, and minimizing losses. By defining risk tolerance levels, implementing stop loss orders, and

adhering to prudent risk-reward ratios, traders can safeguard their funds and enhance their overall risk management practices.

3. Skill Development Goals: Skill development goals aim to improve traders' knowledge, expertise, and competencies in trading by acquiring new skills, enhancing technical analysis proficiency, mastering trading platforms, or staying updated on market trends. Skill development goals empower traders to evolve, adapt, and grow as market participants.

4. Psychological Goals: Psychological goals focus on cultivating emotional resilience, discipline, and mental toughness in trading by managing emotions, controlling impulses, overcoming psychological biases, and maintaining a positive mindset. Psychological goals help

traders navigate the psychological challenges of trading and foster a resilient mindset for long-term success.

Setting Effective Trading Goals

Specific: Define clear and specific trading goals that are well-defined, actionable, and measurable to track progress and evaluate performance effectively.

Achievable: Set realistic and attainable trading goals that align with your skills, resources, and market conditions to ensure feasibility and motivation.

Relevant: Ensure that trading goals are relevant to your trading objectives, strategies, and overarching financial goals to maintain alignment and focus.

Time-bound: Establish timeframes and deadlines for achieving trading goals to create urgency, accountability, and a sense of progress in your trading journey.

By setting trading goals that are focused, achievable, relevant, and time-bound, traders can establish a roadmap for success, stay motivated, and cultivate a disciplined, goal-oriented approach to trading that drives continuous improvement, enhances performance, and maximizes their potential for long-term success in the financial markets.

Creating a Trading Strategy

Creating a trading strategy is a fundamental aspect of successful trading that forms the foundation for making informed decisions, managing risk, and achieving trading objectives in the financial markets. A trading strategy outlines a systematic approach to entering and exiting trades, managing positions, and optimizing risk-reward ratios based on predefined rules, criteria, and analysis methods.

Key Components of a Trading Strategy

1. Market Analysis: A trading strategy begins with thorough market analysis to identify potential opportunities, trends, and market conditions that align with the trader's objectives. Traders can utilize fundamental analysis, technical analysis, and sentiment analysis to assess market dynamics, gauge price movements, and make informed trading decisions.

2. Entry and Exit Rules: Defining clear entry and exit rules is essential in a trading strategy to determine optimal entry points for initiating trades and defining exit points to secure profits or limit losses. Entry rules can be based on technical indicators, chart patterns, fundamental triggers, or a combination of factors, while exit rules can

include stop loss orders, profit targets, trailing stops, or trend reversals.

3. Risk Management: Risk management is a critical component of a trading strategy that involves setting appropriate risk parameters, position sizing, stop loss levels, and risk-reward ratios to protect capital and manage risk exposure effectively. Traders must implement sound risk management practices to safeguard their funds, preserve capital, and optimize their trading performance.

4. Position Sizing: Determining the optimal position size for each trade is an integral part of a trading strategy that considers risk tolerance, account size, leverage, and market conditions. Position sizing techniques, such as fixed dollar amount, percentage of account balance, or

volatility-based sizing, help traders allocate capital judiciously and manage risks while maximizing potential returns.

5. Backtesting and Optimization: Backtesting a trading strategy involves testing its performance on historical data to assess its viability, profitability, and robustness under various market conditions. Traders can optimize their strategies by refining parameters, adjusting settings, and incorporating feedback from backtesting results to enhance performance and adapt to changing market environments.

6. Continuous Monitoring and Evaluation: Monitoring and evaluating the performance of a trading strategy in real-time is essential for identifying strengths, weaknesses, and areas for improvement. Traders should

track key performance metrics, analyze trade outcomes, and adjust their strategies based on market feedback to enhance consistency, profitability, and adaptability.

By incorporating these key components into a comprehensive trading strategy, traders can establish a structured framework for making informed decisions, managing risks, and achieving consistent results in their trading activities. A well-defined trading strategy provides traders with a roadmap for success, a disciplined approach to trading, and a systematic methodology for navigating the complexities of the financial markets with confidence and precision.

Backtesting and Optimization

Backtesting and optimization are vital processes in trading that allow traders to evaluate the performance, robustness, and effectiveness of their trading strategies by analyzing historical data, identifying patterns, and optimizing key parameters to enhance profitability, reduce risk, and improve overall trading performance.

Backtesting

Backtesting involves testing a trading strategy on historical data to assess its viability, profitability, and consistency under various market conditions. Traders use backtesting to simulate trades, analyze performance metrics, and evaluate the effectiveness of their strategies in retrospect. By backtesting a strategy, traders can identify strengths, weaknesses, optimal settings, and potential pitfalls that may arise in different market scenarios.

Benefits of Backtesting

Performance Evaluation: Backtesting allows traders to evaluate the historical performance of their trading strategies to measure profitability, risk-adjusted returns, drawdowns, win rates, and other key metrics.

Strategy Refinement: Analyzing backtesting results helps traders refine, optimize, and fine-tune their strategies by adjusting entry and exit rules, risk management parameters, position sizing techniques, and other critical components.

Risk Mitigation: By backtesting a strategy, traders can assess its risk-reward profile, volatility, maximum drawdown potential, and overall risk exposure to implement robust risk management practices and protect capital effectively.

Optimization

Optimization involves refining and enhancing a trading strategy by adjusting key parameters, variables, and settings based on backtesting results to improve performance, maximize profitability, and adapt to changing market conditions. Traders optimize their strategies to enhance consistency, efficiency, and competitiveness in the dynamic financial markets.

Key Considerations in Optimization

Parameter Sensitivity: Traders need to assess the sensitivity of their strategies to key parameters and test various combinations to find the optimal values that yield the best results during optimization.

Overfitting Avoidance: Traders should be cautious of overfitting their strategies to historical data by optimizing excessively, as this may lead to curve fitting, unrealistic performance, and poor generalization to future market conditions.

Robustness Testing: After optimization, traders should conduct robustness tests by validating their strategies on out-of-sample data, different time periods, market regimes, and asset classes to ensure the strategy's effectiveness across diverse market conditions.

Benefits of Optimization

Enhanced Performance: Optimization helps traders enhance the performance, efficiency, and profitability of their trading strategies by fine-tuning parameters, optimizing settings, and adapting to changing market dynamics.

Adaptability: Optimized strategies are more adaptable, resilient, and flexible in responding to market fluctuations, news events, and evolving trends, allowing traders to capitalize on opportunities and mitigate risks effectively.

Competitive Edge: Optimizing trading strategies gives traders a competitive edge by improving their decision-making process, risk management practices, and overall trading performance compared to market peers.

Backtesting and optimization are essential components of successful trading that enable traders to assess, refine, and enhance their strategies systematically to achieve consistent profitability, mitigate risks, and thrive in the competitive landscape of the financial markets. By incorporating backtesting and optimization processes into their trading routines, traders can optimize their performance, increase their efficiency, and position themselves for long-term success and sustainable growth in their trading endeavors.

Reviewing and Adapting Strategies

Reviewing and adapting trading strategies is a crucial aspect of a trader's journey towards long-term success, as it involves assessing the performance, identifying strengths and weaknesses, and making necessary adjustments to optimize trading outcomes, adapt to changing market conditions, and maintain a competitive edge in the financial markets.

Reviewing Strategies

Reviewing trading strategies involves evaluating past performance, analyzing key metrics, and assessing the effectiveness of the strategy in achieving predefined goals and objectives. Traders review their strategies regularly to identify areas for improvement, understand market dynamics, and make informed decisions based on data-driven insights.

Key Aspects of Reviewing Strategies

Performance Analysis: Traders analyze performance metrics such as return on investment (ROI), win rate, drawdown, risk-adjusted returns, and other key indicators to gauge the effectiveness and profitability of their strategies.

Risk Assessment: Evaluation of risk management practices, risk-reward ratios, maximum drawdowns, and overall risk exposure helps traders assess the resilience of their strategies and identify potential vulnerabilities.

Market Conditions: Understanding how the strategy performed under different market conditions, trends, volatility levels, and economic events provides valuable insights for adapting the strategy to changing environments effectively.

Feedback Loop: Feedback from review processes informs traders about what worked well, what needs improvement, and areas where adjustments are necessary to enhance strategy performance and align with evolving market dynamics.

Adapting Strategies

Adapting trading strategies involves making iterative adjustments, refinements, and enhancements based on the findings from the review process to optimize performance, mitigate risk, and capitalize on market opportunities effectively. Traders adapt their strategies to changing market conditions, emerging trends, and new insights gained from ongoing evaluation and analysis.

Key Considerations in Adapting Strategies

Flexibility: Traders should maintain a flexible approach to adapting strategies by being open to change, exploring new ideas, and adjusting parameters, rules, or techniques to better align with current market conditions.

Iterative Improvement: Continuous refinement and improvement through iterative adaptations allow traders to evolve their strategies, learn from past mistakes, and enhance their decision-making process based on feedback and insights gained from reviews.

Innovation: Encouraging innovation, creativity, and experimentation in adapting strategies helps traders explore new opportunities, test alternative approaches, and stay ahead of market trends by adapting to evolving market landscapes.

Benefits of Reviewing and Adapting Strategies

Enhanced Performance: Regular reviews and adaptations lead to improved performance, increased profitability, and better risk management by fine-tuning strategies to align with market dynamics and trader's goals.

Risk Mitigation: Adapting strategies helps traders mitigate risks, reduce vulnerabilities, and enhance resilience against market uncertainties, unexpected events, and volatility by adjusting to changing conditions effectively.

Competitive Advantage: Continuous adaptation and innovation provide traders with a competitive advantage by staying agile, responsive, and adaptive to market changes, emerging trends, and competitive pressures in the financial markets.

Reviewing and adapting trading strategies are essential processes that enable traders to optimize performance, mitigate risks, and stay competitive in the dynamic and challenging environment of the financial markets. By conducting thorough reviews, embracing continuous improvement, and being proactive in adapting strategies to market developments, traders can position themselves for long-term success, consistency, and profitability in their trading endeavors.

CONCLUSION

The Forex market, a dynamic and ever-evolving landscape, demands a multifaceted approach to navigate its complexities and achieve consistent success. The multitude of available Forex trading strategies, each with its strengths and weaknesses, caters to diverse trading styles, risk tolerances, and time horizons.

Technical analysis, the cornerstone of many strategies, equips traders with tools to decipher market trends, identify support and resistance levels, and pinpoint potential entry and exit points. Trend following strategies capitalize on established market movements, while range trading strategies exploit price fluctuations within defined boundaries. Breakout strategies aim to capture explosive price movements as they pierce through established support or resistance levels, while scalping strategies seek to profit from small, rapid price changes.

Fundamental analysis provides a deeper understanding of the underlying economic forces driving currency valuations. By analyzing economic indicators, geopolitical events, and central bank policies, traders can identify potential imbalances and capitalize on discrepancies between a currency's intrinsic value and its market price. Interest rate differentials, economic growth prospects, and political stability all play crucial roles in shaping currency valuations.

Sentiment analysis delves into the psychology of the market, gauging the overall mood and expectations of market participants. News sentiment analysis, social media monitoring, and sentiment indicators can provide valuable insights into potential shifts in supply and demand dynamics, allowing traders to anticipate market turning points and position themselves accordingly.

Regardless of the chosen strategy, effective risk management is the cornerstone of sustainable Forex trading. Implementing stop-loss orders to limit potential losses, adhering to position sizing techniques to manage exposure, and maintaining a disciplined approach to risk-reward ratios are crucial for protecting capital and ensuring long-term survival in the market.

The ideal Forex trading strategy is not a one-size-fits-all solution but rather a personalized approach tailored to individual preferences, risk tolerance, and time commitment. Evaluating different strategies, backtesting their performance under various market conditions, and continuously refining them to adapt to evolving market dynamics is essential for achieving consistent results.

Ultimately, success in Forex trading hinges on a combination of knowledge, skill, discipline, and a deep understanding of the market's complexities. By embracing continuous learning, developing a robust trading plan, and mastering the art of risk management, traders can increase their odds of navigating the currency maze and achieving their financial goals.

www.ingramcontent.com/pod-product-compliance
Lightning Source LLC
Chambersburg PA
CBHW071058240526
45471CB00016B/2121